Kings and Queens of Southern Africa

Sylviane Anna Diouf

Franklin Watts
A Division of Grolier Publishing
New York • London • Hong Kong • Sydney
Danbury, Connecticut

Note to readers: Definitions for words in **bold** can be found in the Glossary at the back of this book.

Cover illustration by Gary Overacre

Photographs ©: Art Resource, NY: 23 (Manu Sassoonian); Bridgeman Art Library International Ltd., London/New York: 8, 9 (STC89000/A Korah Hottentot Village on the Left Bank of the Orange River. Plate 1 from 'African Scenery and Animals', by Samuel Daniell. 1804. Engraved by the artist. Coloured aquatint. Stapleton Collection), 33 (STC86374/Zulu Blacksmiths at Work. Plate 23 from 'The Kafirs Illustrated', by George French Angas. 1849. Colour lithograph. Stapleton Collection, UK), 45 (STC86370/Zulu Soldiers of King Panda's Army. Plate 20 from 'The Kafirs Illustrated', by George French Angas. 1849. Colour lithograph. Stapleton Collection, UK); Corbis Sygma: 52 (L. Emmanuel); Corbis-Bettmann: 19 bottom, 21, 25, 54 (Francoise de Mulder), 35 (Lindsay Hebberd), 46 (Peter Johnson), 44 (Kim Sayer), 38, 48; Liaison Agency, Inc.: 6, 40 (Pool Raid Gauloise), 12, 13 (David Barritt), 11 (Hadjih Bruno), 51 (Chip Hires), 50 (Hulton Getty), 28 (Frederic Reglain), 14, 22 (Anthony Suau); Mary Evans Picture Library: 19 top (Countries of the World); National Library of South Africa: 3 top, 31, 43; Stock Montage, Inc.: 37, 42; Superstock, Inc.: 16 (Museum for Ethnology, Smpk, Berlin/A.K.G., Berlin), 3 bottom, 26, 27, 29, 36.

Maps by XNR Productions.

Visit Franklin Watts on the Internet at:
http://publishing.grolier.com

Library of Congress Cataloging-in-Publication Data

Diouf, Sylviane Anna
    Kings and queens of Southern Africa / by Sylviane Anna Diouf
       p.   cm.— (Kings and queens of Southern Africa) (Watts Library)
    Includes bibliographical references and index.
    Summary: Surveys historical regions and kingdoms of Southern Africa, with biographies of Nzinga Mbande, Queen of Angola; Shaka, King of the Zulu Nation; and Moshoeshoe, King of the Sotho.
    ISBN 0-531-20374-3 (lib. bdg.)   0-531-16535-3 (pbk.)
    1. Africa, Southern—Kings and rulers—Biography—Juvenile literature. 2. Africa, Southern—History—Juvenile literature. [I. Africa, Southern—Kings and rulers 2. Kings, queens, rulers, etc. 3. Africa, Southern—History.] I. Title. II. Series.
DT1064 .K36 2000
968'.009'9—dc21
                        99-086638

Contents

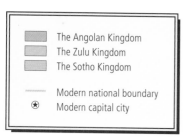

The Angolan Kingdom

The Zulu Kingdom

The Sotho Kingdom

Modern national boundary

Modern capital city

Atlantic Ocean

Luanda

Lake Tanganyika

ANGOLA

MALAWI

ZAMBIA

Lilongwe

Lake Malawi (Lake Nyasa)

Lusaka

Zambezi R.

Harare

ZIMBABWE

MOZAMBIQUE

NAMIBIA

BOTSWANA

KALAHARI DESERT

Windhoek

Gaborone

Pretoria

Mbabane

Maputo

Indian Ocean

LESOTHO

SWAZILAND

Orange R.

Maseru

SOUTH AFRICA

Cape Town

AFRICA

Atlantic Ocean

Area enlarged

Indian Ocean

𝒩

0   500 mi.

0   500 km

Chapter One

Kings and Queens of Africa

Africa is a continent of great natural diversity—burning deserts, snowy mountains, lush forests, dry savannas, and majestic rivers. Africa's 800 million people are as diverse as its landscape. Thousands of different populations live in the continent's fifty-three countries. Africans speak 25 percent of the 6,000 languages that exist on Earth.

For tens of thousands of years, Africans have shared the beauty of this vast continent. The peoples used Africa's immense resources while each population developed its own culture, language, and traditions. This amazing diversity could be a source of richness or of division, but from the earliest times Africa has had great leaders who united diverse communities into strong nations.

The kings and queens of Africa were concerned not only with power and the expansion of their kingdoms, but also with justice, education, arts, crafts, agriculture, and trade.

Some ruled in difficult times. The arrival of the Europeans, the rise of the slave trade, and colonization unsettled their territories and the continent as a whole. Rulers faced external threats and internal divisions, and they had to invent ways to govern and protect their communities.

The rugged landscape of Lesotho, in Southern Africa, protected this region from the population changes that affected most of Southern Africa.

Accounts of the kings and queens of Africa have been passed from one generation to the next through stories and songs. Starting in the eighth century, travelers from North Africa recorded their observations of African rulers in books and letters. Africans, writing in Arabic, did the same, starting in the 1500s. Europeans first arrived in Africa in 1444, and they left records of the rulers and the courts they visited. Natives and foreigners have helped us know the rulers who, with their people, have created the history of Africa.

For the series, *Kings and Queens of Africa*, the continent has been divided into four parts: West, Central, Southern, and East. Each area has characteristics that helped to shape the cultures that developed there. West Africa was a crossroads for trade, and kingdoms and empires based largely on commerce rose in the region. East Africa was molded by the great variety of its peoples. Central Africa was transformed by the migration of the Bantu population from the northwest. Large movements of population changed the course of Southern Africa's history.

Each book in this series looks at different eras to show how the region evolved through time and the most significant rulers of the region. Some were more famous than others, and some well-known figures do not appear here. I have presented social, political, and cultural innovators who connected their kingdoms to a much larger world, defended their territory against foreign invasions, or brought various groups together into one people. These rulers left important legacies.

An eighteenth-century drawing of a village on the banks of the Orange River in Southern Africa

Chapter Two

The Kingdoms of Southern Africa

The history of Southern Africa has been marked by large movements of populations. The first was the Bantu migration. The Bantu people settled in the northern part of the region, in the area of Angola, twenty-five centuries ago. The people were farmers and traders and they introduced the smelting of iron and other metals to the region. In waves, from about the beginning of the sixth century, the Bantu moved south of the Limpopo River.

In the nineteenth century, another vast displacement of population took place. Unlike the Bantu migration, this was swift and brutal and is known as the "crushing" or "hammering." New communities were shaped while others disappeared or relocated. New relationships were forged among clans, chiefdoms, and kingdoms.

Another movement of population came when the Europeans started to settle in Southern Africa in the seventeenth century. They intensified their seizure of land in the nineteenth century.

Angola and the Europeans

When European navigators, traders, and missionaries moved into Southern Africa, its peoples, cultures, and political systems had to adjust. The **Ndongo** kingdom and then the Matamba kingdom, under Queen Nzinga Mbande (1582–1663), struggled to maintain their traditions while contending with the Portuguese and the Dutch slave traders. Nzinga's kingdom was a victim of the slave trade but was also involved in selling captives in exchange for weapons for protection.

Queen Nzinga's story illustrates the difficult choices African rulers had to make. They had to defend themselves against their neighbors and against the European powers. In addition, they were confronted with new religions, weapons, and goods that had important effects on the population.

The Rise of the Zulu

Until the 1820s, the **Zulu** were a minor clan of the Nguni people, but then a series of events led them to prominence. First, they were conquered by Dingiswayo, the **paramount chief** of the **Mthethwa confederacy**. Dingiswayo became a mentor for the Zulu chief Senzangakona. Later, he supported Shaka, (1786–1870), the Zulu king's son, who eventually took control of the confederacy. A strong-willed military genius,

Shaka turned the Zulu and the other clans of the confederacy into a large powerful army. Through conquest, they absorbed other groups and chiefdoms. By 1828, the Zulu kingdom was the strongest and largest in South Africa.

But the **Afrikaner** invasion of the Africans' land and the British colonial rule changed, once again, the social and political landscape of the area. The defeated Zulu, and other black South Africans, had to live for decades under **apartheid**, one of the most brutal policies of the twentieth century.

From the Sotho Kingdom to Lesotho

Caught in the middle of the "hammering," the **Sotho** people, under the leadership of Moshoeshoe, chose a defensive position. King Moshoeshoe's strategy was to take refuge in a remote area that was difficult to reach and easy to defend. Then he rallied the groups who had lost their territory and their hopes. Like the Zulu kingdom, the Sotho kingdom emerged only after the vast population movements that reshaped Southern Africa.

The **Basotho** (the plural of Sotho) and some Nguni clans united by Moshoeshoe fought a successful defensive war, and the kingdom was able to gain independence. But Moshoeshoe and the Basotho were ultimately betrayed by the Europeans, who seized a large part of their land.

The Zulu are still active. This photograph shows the Zulu celebrating the coronation of King Mswati in 1986.

13

This part of Angola, south of Luanda, shows that the landscape can make travel difficult.

Chapter Three

Nzinga Mbande, Queen of Angola

Nzinga Mbande and her attendants had been walking for a long time. Weeks earlier, they had started out from Kabasa, the capital of the **Ndongo** kingdom in northern Angola.

Mbundu and Ndongo

The **Mbundu** people, who speak a Bantu language, Kimbundu, came from eastern Africa and settled in northern Angola. In Nzinga's time, the Mbundu were farmers, crafts-people, and long-distance traders. the western Mbundu were some-times called the Ndongo. The king-dom of Ndongo, *Ngola a Kiluanje*, was the largest kingdom of the Mbundu. When it was defeated in the sixteenth century, western Ndongo fell under Portuguese control as part of the *conquista*, and eastern Ndongo became part of the kingdom of Matamba.

A sixteenth-century wooden sculpture of a Portuguese soldier

Princess Nzinga was determined. Her mission was of great importance for her people, the Mbundu. She was going to meet the Portuguese governor, who resided in Luanda, a city on the Atlantic Coast of Africa.

The Portuguese first arrived in this part of Africa at the end of the fifteenth century and seized some Angolan land. They called it **conquista**, or conquered territory. They claimed it as part of Portugal, and the king of Portugal appointed a military governor to rule over it. The governors served three-year terms.

From Luanda, the Portuguese capital of the conquista built in 1576, they conducted trade with the Angolans. Their main interest was to acquire men, women, and children. The Portuguese then shipped the Angolans overseas to work as slaves on plantations in the Americas.

The Rise of the Slave Trade

As Princess Nzinga walked across the plains, going through villages and small towns, talking to her people, she heard the same complaints over and over again. The Mbundu were treated cruelly by the Portuguese. Their land was taken, and people kidnapped and sent into slavery overseas. The year was 1622 and Nzinga was forty. All her life she had faced insecurity and war brought by the Portuguese.

In 1579, her father, the **ngola**, or king, had ordered that all the Portuguese living at his court be killed because he feared that Portugal was going to conquer his land. By 1582, when Nzinga was born, the ngola had been fighting the invaders for three years.

The wars, the raids, and the fear of the slave traders weakened the kingdom of Ndongo and many neighboring kingdoms. The people who were the most affected were the Mbundu, a large, widespread, and peaceful population.

The Portuguese, to subdue the Mbundu, allied themselves with the Imbangala, another Angolan people. The Imbangala were nomad warriors who lived mostly by attacking and stealing from the Mbundu and other settled peoples.

The Portuguese and the Imbangala began a series of battles against the Mbundu. After each battle, all captured Mbundu men and women were shipped to South American and Caribbean plantations, where they spent their lives as slaves. But the Mbundu were fierce fighters and often repelled the invaders.

When Nzinga was nine, in 1591, the Mbundu stopped a Portuguese and Imbangala invasion. A second Portuguese campaign followed and, again, failed. In 1597, they launched a third campaign, and defeated the Mbundu. But the war was not over yet. It continued for decades.

A Mission for Nzinga

In 1617, Nzinga's father died. His successor was his son, Mbandi. Mbandi, a weak man, resisted attacks but never launched an offensive. When the Portuguese and their Imbangala allies attacked his capital, Kabasa, he fled and left it undefended. The Portuguese burned down Kabasa and laid the region to waste. The Mbundu now faced widespread famine.

Broken, Mbandi thought it was time to make peace. He needed a treaty with the Portuguese governor in Luanda. But who could he send? Who would appear strong enough so that the enemy would agree to negotiate a peace and thus prevent another war? Who could be firm enough to win the best conditions for the Mbundu? His choice could only be Nzinga Mbande, his older sister, a woman of strong will, courage, and pride.

After the long trek, Nzinga arrived in Luanda and was brought into the governor's chamber. She saw that he was sitting in a comfortable chair, but there was no chair for her. As she negotiated the future of her people, she would have to stand, like a servant of this governor. But she was the daughter and sister of kings, the equal of any governor. Nzinga set out to

Luanda

Luanda has remained Angola's capital. Today, it has 2 million inhabitants.

This nineteenth-century drawing of Luanda shows that the city developed near the water.

Today, Luanda is Angola's largest city and chief port and industrial center.

show him that she was given more respect and obedience by her people than he received. Nzinga Mbande raised her hand, and one of her servants came to her and knelt down. Nzinga sat on the servant's back. The governor was stunned and realized that this woman would not be easy to intimidate. The princess described the Mbundu of the Ndongo kingdom as well-armed and prepared to fight, even though they had been defeated. When the meeting ended, Nzinga had gained an honorable peace for her people.

During her stay in Luanda, Nzinga observed the Portuguese and understood that if she became a Christian it would help her gain their trust. She was baptized and became a Catholic, taking the name Anna da Souza.

Nzinga Comes to Power

Back in her kingdom, Nzinga was welcomed as a hero. The popularity of the weak Ngola Mbandi, however, was sinking. In 1624, he died. Nzinga became the regent because Mbandi's son was too young to govern. But the forty-two-year-old woman wanted to reign in her own name, not as a regent who would have to hand over power in a few years. In 1626, with a cruelty perhaps based on her determination to protect her people, she ordered her nephew killed. Nzinga Mbande became the ruler.

From the start, Nzinga insisted on using the title *ngola*, which had been reserved for men. She also went back to the religion of her people. She surrounded herself with women

Angolan Women

Traditionally, Angolan women form strong kinship groups. They support one another and play an important part in social and political life. For a long time, women were the suppliers of the Angolan kingdom's currency, the *nzimbu* shells. Female divers brought them up from the waters of the Bay of Luanda.

bodyguards, and she reorganized the army, creating female regiments. In 1627, her first year as the ngola, she launched an attack on the Portuguese using a formation of three groups of warriors. She led one, while her sisters Mukambu and Kifunji led the others. It was unusual for women to lead the army and amazing for a queen to take part personally in a battle. But Nzinga Mbande was always independent and strong.

Led by the three sisters, the Mbundu warriors closed in on the Portuguese. They were sure of their victory when they suddenly saw the cavalry, hidden behind a knoll. Horses had been introduced into Southern Africa by the Europeans, but the people in Nzinga's area were not familiar with the animals. The horses gave the Portuguese a strong advantage. To avoid a massacre, Nzinga order her troops to retreat. Unfortunately, her two sisters were captured and spent long years in prison in Luanda. Emboldened by their victory, the Portuguese launched new attacks on the Mbundu and killed thousands.

Nzinga vowed to continue fighting, but her people were suffering. Unable to ensure their safety, Nzinga decided to move her whole nation into another territory. The Mbundu would leave the plains of Ndongo and would settle east, in the highlands of Matamba, a kingdom they had conquered. There they could defend themselves better.

Nzinga moved her people inland, to a highland region. Today, areas of the Angolan hills are dotted with coffee plantations.

A New Land

The long march started in 1630 and lasted five years. Every man, woman, and child—including the elderly, sick, and wounded—and their cattle, walked for hundreds of miles across the plains, the rivers, and the hills. The baggage of an entire nation was carried over miles and miles of forests and difficult terrain.

Nzinga Mbande was now the ruler of the Matamba kingdom. She continued

In Angolan culture, women have always been powerful. This traditional Angolan mask of the Chokwe people represents a female ancestor.

to fight the Portuguese, trying to rally other kingdoms. In the 1640s, she waged three successful campaigns against the Portuguese and allied herself with their European enemies, the Dutch. The Dutch had opened trading posts on the coast as rivals of the Portuguese. They too were involved in the slave trade. With the support of the Dutch, Nzinga became powerful. Part of her power came from the slave trade. Nzinga sold prisoners of war to the Dutch to get firearms and ammunition for protection. When her allies, the Dutch, conquered Luanda in 1640, Nzinga made Matamba the most powerful kingdom in the area.

In 1648, Nzinga's old enemies, the Portuguese, retook Luanda. This time, she decided to accept their presence as long as it did not threaten her independence and safety. In 1650, at age sixty-eight, she returned to Catholicism and asked the pope to send missionaries. She welcomed Portuguese officials at her court, built churches and schools, and abolished **polygamy** and human sacrifice.

The Legacy of Nzinga

In 1663, at age eighty-one, Nzinga Mbande died. She was deeply mourned by the people she had led for thirty-seven difficult years. Nzinga left her kingdom of Matamba powerful and independent. Her bravery and concern for her people gained their respect, and the kingdom accepted numerous other female rulers until the beginning of the twentieth century. Matamba then fell under Portuguese colonial rule, along

with the rest of Angola. The country regained its independence through another war against the Portuguese, which ended in 1974.

Nzinga Mbande was a proud and effective ruler, with courage and moral strength. She could also be cruel and take drastic actions when she felt she had to. She knew when to make alliances, and when to resist or attack. As one of the first fighters for independence, she remains a hero for the people of Angola. She is also a model for Angolan women. She has remained a beloved and admired figure not only in Angola but throughout Africa.

The women of Angola, like Nzinga, have been strong fighters for independence.

The landscape of Zululand, Shaka's kingdom

Chapter Four

Shaka, King of the Zulu Nation

Young Nandi was desperate. Although not married, she was expecting a child. The father was Senzangakona, a Zulu prince who was a distant relative. In Natal, the southern African land where she lived, this was considered a serious offense by the Nguni people. Her family ordered her to go by herself to announce the news to the future father. Nandi

The Ndebele are a clan of the Nguni people. In Ndebele villages, the homes are painted with bright patterns.

walked to his town, but before she could see him, an elder of his clan stopped her and asked her why she was coming. Nandi explained her mission. The elder mocked her and said that perhaps she was not really pregnant, that there was a *shaka* (beetle) in her belly. Humiliated, the young woman returned home, where a few months later, she gave birth to a boy amid the shame of her family. She named him Shaka.

A Bitter Life

Soon afterward, Nandi's family sent her and the child, Shaka, to stay with Senzangakona. Since she came with a child, the young woman became Senzangakona's third wife, but she was denied the honor of a ceremonial wedding. Her husband paid her little attention, and his other wives disliked her.

Amid her unhappiness, one joyful event took place. She gave birth to a daughter, Nomcoba. Young Shaka was delighted to have a baby sister, and Nomcoba remained his best friend all his life. Nandi, Shaka, and Nomcoba led an unhappy but secure existence, until one day, when they were told to leave. Tradition says that this happened because one of the sheep tended by the six-year-old Shaka had died. His father, who had little love for the boy or his mother, used this incident as an excuse to get rid of them.

This photo shows the traditional dome-shaped and tightly woven Zulu huts. Shaka probably grew up in a similar hut.

Returning to Her People

Nandi and her two children went back to her family. There, life was difficult for Shaka. His illegitimate birth was considered shamful. As the son of a prince, he had enjoyed a high status when living with his father, but now the other youngsters taunted him about his birth. They mocked him because after living as the son of a prince, he was now in a lower rank. He had nobody to defend him but his mother. They also teased him because of his great height. Shaka was humiliated, beaten, and insulted. But the experience made him stronger. He learned how to fight back and gained confidence.

Unwelcome, Shaka and his family moved from one place to another until they finally settled in the home of Nandi's aunt, among the Mthethwa. There Shaka spent the happiest years of his childhood. He became a trusted and strong herdser, and while tending cattle, he developed his fighting skills. He used hunting **assagais** as weapons instead of the heavier spears of the soldiers. He was now fifteen, and along with all other boys his age, he had to serve six years of military service.

The Mthethwa Confederacy

Shaka became an excellent soldier and caught the attention of the ruler, Dingiswayo, the **paramount chief** of the Mthethwa confederacy. Through war, Dingiswayo had united a number of small states—including the Zulu state led by Shaka's father, Senzangakona—and other states and clans that paid him tribute. Dingiswayo was impressed with Shaka and wanted to reunite him with his father. He invited Senzangakona to come to meet Shaka. When the Zulu king saw the young soldier, he did not recognize him but was impressed by his skills. Senzangakona asked who this fine young man was. "I am Shaka," responded his son, bitter at his father's past indifference. Shaka walked away.

In 1816, Senzangakona died. The Zulu council wanted Shaka to become his successor, but one of Senzangakona's wives had convinced the dying ruler to nominate another son, Sigujana. Shaka was angry and determined to use any means—however cruel—to be the new Zulu leader. He thought up a scheme to get rid of competition from his other brothers and to be recognized as the new chief. He persuaded one of his half-brothers to kill Sigujana. Mysteriously, the murderer himself was then killed.

Shaka, ruler of the Zulu nation

Shaka the King

Shaka became king of the Zulu nation in 1816. He chose a new capital, which he called *Kwa Bulawayo* (the place of killing). And soon it would be exactly that—a place where much blood

The Zulu

Before Shaka's reign, the Zulu, numbering only 1,500, were the smallest clan of the Nguni people. Other Nguni clans include the Swazi, **Ndebele**, Xhosa, and Pondo.

was shed. When Shaka took power, the Zulu nation was a small state. He was determined to make it the strongest and the most important state in the region. But first, he had to reorganize the army, which by tradition included men and women. With a better army, he could conquer new territories and subdue other kingdoms.

Shaka set out to toughen his soldiers and teach them to obey his commands. He had the large square in Kwa Bulawayo littered with hard thorns. Then he ordered the soldiers to walk across the square barefoot. Those who refused or even hesitated were pulled aside and killed. Shaka's brutality gained prompt obedience. Through terror, he shaped the men and women into a disciplined, strong force. With their hardened feet, the Zulu could fight barefoot, and they were faster than their enemies.

His next step was to build endurance in his soldiers. They marched for 30 miles (48 km) without food. After arriving at their destination, they were sent back to the starting point. This training prepared the Zulu soldiers to march for more than 50 miles (80 km) and be ready for battle. Shaka himself was tireless. One day, he walked 50 miles (80 km) to see a relative. Without resting, he walked another 30 miles (48 km) to pay respect to the chief of the confederacy, Dingiswayo.

The third part of Shaka's strategy was to provide the soldiers with better weapons. Shaka used his experience with the hunting assagai to create a new type of weapon—a stabbing spear that required the warrior to get close to the enemy. To do that, a soldier needed a special shield to protect his or her entire body. Shaka designed a body-length shield made of hard cowhide. Hidden behind their black-and-white shields, the Zulu warriors were protected from the enemy's spears.

Shaka was the commander in chief of an army of 60,000 men and 10,000 women. Historians have said that it was the best trained and most efficient army in Africa. The Zulu had many victories, conquering their neighbors. They turned the prisoners they took in battle into soldiers, incorporating them into the Zulu army and the Zulu nation.

The Zulu have been skilled blacksmiths for many generations. They used their knowledge of metal to forge weapons.

Mfecane

Bantu peoples started to settle in Southern Africa, where they lived in small states, between A.D. 500 and 1000. In the nineteenth century, a revolution of enormous proportions took place. It is known as **mfecane** (crushing) in Nguni languages and as **difaqane** (hammering) in Sesotho. The revolution was due to a population increase that led to a land shortage, plus a severe drought in 1806. In addition, the development of trade between the northern Nguni and Portugal created competition among the Bantu states. Wars, raids, and conquests ravaged the region. Weaker states disappeared, and powerful nations were created. People regrouped in certain areas, while other areas lost their population. White settlers took the opportunity to seize the land. The mfecane completely changed the region and, some historians believe, left the African populations unprepared to face the white settlers' invasion. But the revolution also gave rise to strong communities such as the Sotho, the Zulu, and the Swazi. They gathered and absorbed diverse and once-rival populations.

The Zulu Nation

When his old protector Dingiswayo was killed in 1818, Shaka became the paramount chief of the Mthethwa confederacy. Since his goal was to make the Zulu nation the most important force in the region, he incorporated the confederacy into his Zulu state. Shaka and his fearless army waged many battles, but often they did not have to fight. Neighboring chiefdoms and clans offered allegiance, not wanting to fight this army whose fame had spread through the region.

For years, the whole area of Southern Africa was in turmoil, due to a huge growth in population, a land shortage, and climate changes that affected the crops and led to famine. Some states, like the Zulu state, became aggressive and conquered land. Others, like the Sotho state, relied on defense. During this period, the Zulu expanded their territory. Entire populations fled before them. Villages and towns were destroyed. Landless farmers became nomads and then preyed on weaker clans.

The Crushing

The Zulu called this series of events the *mfecane*, which means the "crushing." One strategy used by Shaka during the mfecane was to destroy land to create a desert zone with no resources. He wanted to discourage the European colonists who had settled in the South from crossing the desolate zone to penetrate his territory.

During her son's climb to power, Nandi remained in her village. Shaka gave her much authority, but she did not want to use it.

The Zulu were known as fierce warriors, but they are also renowned for their crafts, such as these finely made baskets.

Zulu shields are still made in the traditional style for ceremonial purposes.

In her village home, she prayed for the well-being and success of her son. The Zulu king was attached to his mother, who had suffered much. Nandi had always protected her children, and now it was Shaka's turn to ensure that her life was sheltered and pleasant.

In October 1827, news reached the Zulu king that his mother was sick. Shaka jumped on his horse and raced to her village. She was very ill and within a few moments, the courageous Nandi, the woman who had stood by her children in dishonor and hard times, died. The one parent who had known and loved Shaka his entire life was gone.

A British friend of Shaka who was there with him described the scene: "For about twenty minutes, Shaka stood in a silent, mournful attitude with his head bowed upon his shield on which I saw large tears fall, occasionally wiping them away with his right hand. After two or three deep sighs . . . he broke out into frantic yells."

A Time of Terror

Shaka, the fearless, pitiless warrior, was completely crushed. His despair destroyed any humanity and compassion he had. The grieving son turned into a terrifying, insane monster. He ordered those who, according to him or his court, did not show enough emotion at Nandi's death to be executed. Two months of senseless cruelty and countless deaths followed.

Despite earlier episodes of cruelty, the Zulu people had admired and obeyed their legendary leader, but this terrible episode turned them against him. They were still obedient, out of terror, but their hearts were no longer with him. His ambitious half-brothers, Dingaan and Mhlangaan, felt that perhaps it was time to get rid of him.

On September 22, 1828, almost one year after Nandi's death, Shaka was sitting, as was his custom, under a wild fig tree. He was looking at the Indian Ocean on one side and the hills of his country on the other. Some traders came, bringing blue crane feathers that were valued by the Zulu. He did not like them and sent the men away. Meanwhile, his half-brothers hid behind a fence, and when the traders left, they ran up to Shaka. Their short

A nineteenth-century journalist illustrated the scene of Dingaan's attack against the Boers in 1838.

From Dutch to Afrikaner

In 1652, the Dutch East India Company opened a station at the Cape of Good Hope to provide supplies to ships on their way to Asia. It encouraged the settlement of Dutch, French, and Germans, called Boers ("farmers" in Dutch) or Afrikaners. The settlers seized the Africans' land, enslaved them, and established their own states when the British took control of the country in 1795.

In 1948, the Afrikaners created the racist policy of **apartheid**. This policy denied the most basic rights to black South Africans—75 percent of the population. Before the policy was ended in 1990, apartheid was directed at segregating the races, as reflected by this street bench reserved for use by Europeans (whites) only. The person ignoring the restriction could have been arrested.

stabbing spears were hidden beneath their cloaks. Mhlangaan stabbed first. He aimed for the heart, but the king wore a coarse leopard-skin cloak on which the spear slid, and his weapon hit Shaka's arm. Twice more the brothers stabbed him, but he managed to pull away. Finally, Dingaan and Mhlangaan plunged their spears into their half-brother's body. Shaka fell to the ground. The great Zulu king was dead.

Hard Times

Dingaan succeeded Shaka. His reign was the most difficult in the history of the Zulu nation. The desert zone that Shaka had created, hoping to keep the Europeans from entering his territory, attracted them instead. The *Voortrekker* were groups of Afrikaners who wanted to establish a colony independent of the British settlers. The Voortrekkers thought that since nobody was living there, they could take the land and build farms. In 1837, the Voortrekkers moved into Zulu territory. Dingaan attacked them and razed their city of Port Natal to the ground. But in December 1838, the settlers used a cannon against the Zulu warriors and destroyed their forces at a river that has been known ever since as Blood River. It was the worst defeat ever experienced by the army built by Shaka.

Shaka's ruthless cruelty is not to be forgotten, but he is also remembered as one of the greatest army chiefs of all time. Shaka the Zulu created the strongest army in Africa. An able political leader, he united clans, chiefdoms, and small kingdoms into the most powerful state in Southern Africa.

A Zulu Defeat

In 1828, Shaka refused to let his army rest and sent it on an expedition to Mozambique. It was defeated. This last failure prompted his half-brothers to quickly get rid of the leader.

In Moshoeshoe's day, cattle were very important. Today, people who live in the same region also raise sheep.

Chapter Five

Moshoeshoe, King of the Sotho

Hidden in the bushes, young Lepoqo was watching the beautiful cattle grazing peacefully. For the Sotho people of Southern Africa, cattle were the most valuable goods. To have cattle was a sign of wealth and power. Cattle breeding and cattle raiding were the two most important activities of Sotho men. To be recognized as a man, a young Sotho had to

Sotho

Sotho means "light black" or "dark brown," probably a reference to the color of the people. The Sotho people (or the Basotho, the plural form) settled in Southern Africa more than a thousand years ago. Their language, Sesotho, belongs to the Bantu group. They grow millet, sorghum, and maize, and keep cattle and goats. Traditionally, they pass on their history through songs, stories, proverbs, riddles, and poems.

steal somebody's cattle and bring the herd, undetected, to his home village. Lepoqo, the eldest son of a **petty chief**, was determined to make his first exploit as a warrior a great success. He chose to raid the cattle of a neighboring chief, Ramonaheng.

When he successfully drove the herd through his village, Lepoqo told the elders that he had shaved off Chief Ramonaheng's beard, meaning that he had taken something personal and valuable in a skillful manner. That day, he chose for himself the name *Moshoeshoe*, the "shaver." The name (pronounced Mo-shwesh-way) imitates the sound a razor blade makes when pulled along the skin.

Moshoeshoe's Refuge

Moshoeshoe was born in 1786, the same year as Shaka. The lives of the Sotho chief and his people were influenced by the actions of the Zulu king.

By 1820, the impact of the social, military, and political turmoil that the Bosotho called the *difaqane* or "hammering" (called the *mfecane* by the Zulu) was felt all over Southern Africa. Displaced populations roamed the land, and refugees regrouped and started wars against settled people. There were constant raids and warfare. Moshoeshoe, who succeeded his father, had the responsibility of protecting his people. In contrast to the agressive Shaka, Moshoeshoe thought defense was the best policy for his people.

Moshoeshoe, king of Lesotho

He looked for a place so difficult to reach and so easy to defend that the Basotho would be left in peace. After scouting the region, he chose a 1,235-acre (499-ha) plateau atop a steep peak. He ordered stone walls to be erected around it and sent watchmen and soldiers to guard the walls. When the enemy approached, the Basotho were warned by the sentinels and

43

could ready themselves for action. Moshoeshoe called his refuge *Thaba Bosiu*, meaning "the mountain climbed at night."

Thaba Bosiu was attacked many times, but its location was so secure that nobody succeeded. Its reputation for safety drew many refugees. Moshoeshoe gathered all the groups into a single nation. He gave hope and restored the spirit of people whose lives were disrupted, their land taken, and their communities scattered.

One of the clans he welcomed introduced horses to the new nation. The horses gave the Basotho mobility and speed, and they soon became excellent riders. They bred their own race of horses, called Basotho ponies.

The Basotho ponies, introduced during Moshoeshoe's time, are still used by his descendants today.

A Peaceful Kingdom

Moshoeshoe sought alliances with other nations and gave them land around Thaba Bosiu to create buffer zones between the Basotho and their rivals. The king was a good leader and ensured his kingdom's safety by defending it, attacking some states when necessary, and befriending others.

Once, the Ndebele army attacked Thaba Bosiu but was beaten back. As they retreated, Moshoeshoe sent a herd of cattle and a messenger after them. He told them that the Sotho king wanted peace and that he understood the Ndebele had invaded because they were hungry. Therefore, he was sending them the herd as a gift. Cattle were valuable. The Ndebele appreciated Moshoeshoe's generosity and never again attacked.

Moshoeshoe also wanted good relations with Shaka, so he sent him a tribute of precious blue crane feathers. By 1834, Moshoeshoe

The prized blue crane feathers can be seen in the headdress of the Zulu soldiers at the left.

Today, Protestants and Catholics make up 80 percent of the population.

ruled over 25,000 people who were grateful to their leader for their peace and security. Eventually more than 250,000 Basotho lived in Moshoeshoe's kingdom, united by his leadership.

The French Arrive

In 1833, the Sotho king heard of the arrival of French Protestant missionaries who were said to be people of peace. He invited them to join the Basotho. The French founded a mission near Thaba Bosiu, and one of them became Moshoeshoe's secretary and interpreter. The king appointed a missionary to each of his subordinate chiefs. By 1847, there were nine missions among the Basotho, each one with a school.

The French missionaries baptized and converted several of Moshoeshoe's aides, and some of his relatives, including a few wives and sons. As he knew that polygamy was not accepted by the Protestant Church, the Sotho king granted divorces to his wives who had become

Christians. But he never converted and continued to defend polygamy and his traditional religion.

The French missionaries advised Moshoeshoe on his relations with the Europeans. The king reasoned that since more and more white settlers were coming to the region, he had to be able to communicate with their leaders in Europe, in case the colonists made trouble. He allowed European traders to set up stores near his city. They bought cattle, millet, wheat, and corn from the Basotho and sold them firearms, ammunition, and metal utensils. To control traders coming from Europe or from farther south, Moshoeshoe forbade them to acquire land in his kingdom.

Afrikaners

Meanwhile, the Afrikaners, descendants of Dutch, French, and German settlers, were becoming threatening. They defeated Dingaan, the Zulu king who had succeeded Shaka, and took possession of parts of Zululand. The Afrikaners then moved toward the Sotho kingdom. Moshoeshoe sought to ally himself with the British, who did not seem to want his territory. In 1843, he signed a treaty with the British governor of the Cape Colony. The treaty recognized the Sotho king as ruler of all the land between the Orange and the Caledon Rivers. But in 1848, a new governor seized the land between the Orange and the Vaal Rivers, including part of Moshoeshoe's territory. Soon border disputes arose between the Basotho and the European settlers.

Cape Colony

The Cape Colony of South Africa was founded by the Dutch East India Company and was taken over by the British in 1795.

Moshoeshoe's forces attack the British infantry in 1851.

In 1850, the British mounted an expedition against Moshoeshoe. The British governor demanded 10,000 cattle, knowing this demand would mean war. He was determined to wipe out the Sotho kingdom, but when he saw well-fortified Thaba Bosiu, he realized that the battle would be costly for both sides. Moshoeshoe understood that too. In his typical manner—to avoid bloodshed and to maintain good relations with a country he might need later—the Sotho king allowed the battle to go on for just one day. He then gave 3,000 cattle to the British, who left with their dignity intact.

A Peaceful King's Words

War "was commenced by the Boers in massacring my people. . . . Poor people, they thought their honesty and love for Christianity would be a shield for them, and that the white people would attack in the first place, if they attacked at all, those who they said were thieves. I ordered my people then all to retreat toward my residence, and left the fury of the Boers [to] be spent upon an empty land; unfortunately some skirmishes took place, some Boers were killed, some of my people also. . . . I will speak of many Basutos who were taken prisoners by the Whites and then killed, most cruelly. . . . My bands were getting ready to make a descent upon them, when the Boers thought proper to make request for a cessation of hostilities. I knew what misery I should bring upon my country by leaving the Basutos to ravage the Boer places. . . . If [the Basotho] have remained quiet, it has been owing to my persuasions and my promises that they might have good hope of justice."

—An 1858 letter from King Moshoeshoe to the British authorities

In 1854, Great Britain decided to pull out of the area. The British left the Basotho to face the Afrikaners. A war broke out between the Afrikaners and the Basotho in 1858 and then again in 1865.

The Afrikaners who established a settlement in the west—the Orange Free State—raided the Basotho, killing their cattle, destroying their crops, and burning down their villages. They tried to enter Thaba Bosiu, but once again Moshoeshoe was able to push them back. The Basotho, for their part, retaliated against the Afrikaners. Moshoeshoe's people continued to resist even after some of their petty chiefs signed treaties with the Europeans.

Lesotho

Lesotho is a monarchy with a national assembly and a senate. A large proportion of its 2 million inhabitants, mostly the men, work in South Africa. A 1947 photo- graph shows Lesotho under British rule. The regent lived in the Euro- pean-style building in the back- ground, surrounded by the huts of the Lesotho people.

From Basutoland to Lesotho

To contain the Afrikaners, the aging Moshoeshoe again sought help from Great Britain, which responded by declaring the country a British protectorate to stop the Afrikaners from incorporating it into the Orange Free State. Moshoeshoe's country became Basutoland in 1868. Without informing him, the British and the Afrikaners carved up his land between

them and left the Basotho only a small enclave. Moshoeshoe died two years later, on March 11, 1870, at eighty-four.

Moshoeshoe's country gained independence from Great Britain in 1966 and took the name Lesotho. Because its fertile land had been seized, it is heavily dependent on South Africa, which surrounds it on all sides.

Lesotho lives on, due to the strength of Moshoeshoe, who saved his country from disintegration and from absorption by the Orange Free State. The wise and widely respected founder of Lesotho, a peace-loving man who had to wage wars to enjoy peace, lives on through his sons, who have held power since the great king's death.

King Letsie III of Lesotho (center), with a visitor, the king of Swaziland (left), in 1997

The political scene in South Africa is active. Here a speaker bullhorns his message to the crowd at a political rally.

Chapter Six

Southern Africa Today

The European impact was strongly felt in Southern Africa even more than in the rest of the African continent. Countries such as Angola, South-West Africa (Namibia), South Africa, and Rhodesia (Zimbabwe) were settlement colonies. Portuguese, Dutch, French, German, and British people settled there and—even though small minorities—kept the African populations in complete subjection. Eventually, in all these countries, the Africans recovered their rights through armed struggle.

Independence Day in Angola

Nevertheless, racism, discrimination, and segregation, which prevailed for so long, left their mark on the region. This has been particularly true in South Africa. Democracy was not established in South Africa until 1994, when all citizens gained the right to vote.

With the exception of Lesotho and Swaziland, which are monarchies, all the other countries of the southern part of Africa are republics with elected presidents. But the kings and queens of yesterday have not been forgotten.

Queen Nzinga was an inspiration for the Angolans fighting for their independence from Portugal. Shaka continues to symbolize the pride and strength of the Zulu people. And even today, Moshoeshoe's descendants rule the kingdom that their ancestor created and protected.

Glossary

Afrikaner—a white descendant of Dutch settlers in South Africa

allegiance—the loyalty and obligations of a lesser king or state to a more powerful one

apartheid—the separation of the races

assagai—a short, lightweight spear, traditionally used for hunting

Basotho—see Sotho

conquista—Angolan territory conquered in the sixteenth century and administered by the Portuguese

difaqane—a Sotho word meaning "hammering" that describes the same events as the Zulu word, *mfecane*

Mbundu—a people living in northern Angola

mfecane—a Nguni word meaning "crushing." It is used to describe the political, social, and military upheaval that took place in nineteenth-century Southern Africa.

Mthethwa confederacy—a group of small states united through war

Ndebele—a Nguni group, who live mainly in Zimbabwe. A smaller number live in South Africa.

Ndongo—an ancient kingdom in northern Angola

ngola—ruler of the Mbundu people. The name *Angola* comes from *ngola*.

paramount chief—the supreme leader who oversees all lower chiefs or kings

petty chief—a chief of inferior rank

polygamy—the practice of allowing a man (and occasionally a woman) to have more than one spouse at the same time

Sotho—one of the largest groups of people in southern Africa. *Basotho* is the plural term.

Zulu—a people living in South Africa

To Find Out More

Books

Bessire, Mark. *Great Zimbabwe*. Danbury, CT: Franklin Watts, 1999.

Blauer, Ettagale and Jason Lauré. *South Africa*. Danbury, CT: Children's Press, 1998.

Klopper, Sandra. *The Zulu Kingdom*. Danbury, CT, Franklin Watts, 1999.

Mann, Kenny. *Monomotapa, Zulu, Basuto: Southern Africa*. Parsippany, NJ: Dillon, 1996.

McKee, Timothy Saunders. *No More Strangers Now: Young Voices from a New South Africa*. New York: DK Publishing, 1998.

McKissack, Patricia. *Nzingha, Warrior Queen of Matamba Angola, Africa 1595*. New York: Scholastic, 2000.

Middleton, Nick. *Southern Africa*. Austin, TX: Raintree Steck-Vaughn, 1995.

Stanley, Diane and Peter Vennema. *Shaka: King of the Zulus*. Mulberry Books, 1994.

Wilson-Max, Ken. *Halala Means Welcome: A Book of Zulu Words*. New York: Hyperion, 1998.

Organizations and Online Sites

African American Cultural Alliance
P.O. Box 22173
Nashville, TN 37202
This group promotes African culture through educational programs and the performing arts.

African Art Museum of Maryland
5430 Vantage Point Road
Columbia, MD 21044
See art and cultural objects of Africa in this museum.

The DuSable Museum of African-American History
740 East 56th Place
Chicago, IL 60637-1495
http://www.dusablemuseum.org/
This museum collects, preserves, and interprets artifacts and information related to African and African-American history and culture.

Homowo Foundation for African Arts and Culture
2915 NE 15th Avenue
Portland, OR 97202
This organization promotes African culture through the performing arts.

The Museum of African American History
315 East Warren at Bush Street
Detroit, MI 48201
http://www.maah-detroit.org/
Learn about African and African-American history and culture by visiting this museum or its website.

Research Institute of African and African American Diaspora Arts
12 Morley Street
Roxbury, MA 02119
This institute conducts research and provides educational programs on African culture.

A Note on Sources

I consulted a variety of sources for *Kings and Queens of Southern Africa*. In particular: *The General History of Africa* (eight volumes), published by UNESCO and the University of California Press; *Encyclopedia of Africa South of the Sahara* (four volumes), John Middleton, ed.; *African History from Earliest Times to Independence* by Philip Curtin et al; *Queen Nzinga:The Woman Who Saved Her People* by David Sweetman; *South Africa: A Modern History* by T. R. H. Davenport; *Shaka, King of the Zulu: The Herd-Boy who Founded a Nation* by Richard Woolley; *African Kingdoms* by Lucy Mair Clarendon; and *Warrior Chiefs of Southern Africa* by Ian J. Knight.

—*Sylviane Anna Diouf*

Index

Numbers in *italics* indicate illustrations.

About the Author

Sylviane Anna Diouf is the author of fiction and nonfiction books for adults and children and of numerous articles for international publications. She specializes in the history of Africa and of people of African origin.

Of Senegalese and French parentage, Ms. Diouf has lived in various African and European countries and in the United States. She has traveled in many parts of the world, and speaks several languages. She holds a doctorate from the University of Paris and lives in New York City with her son.